BIOMIMICRY

AWESOME INNOVATIONS
INSPIRED BY
PLANTS

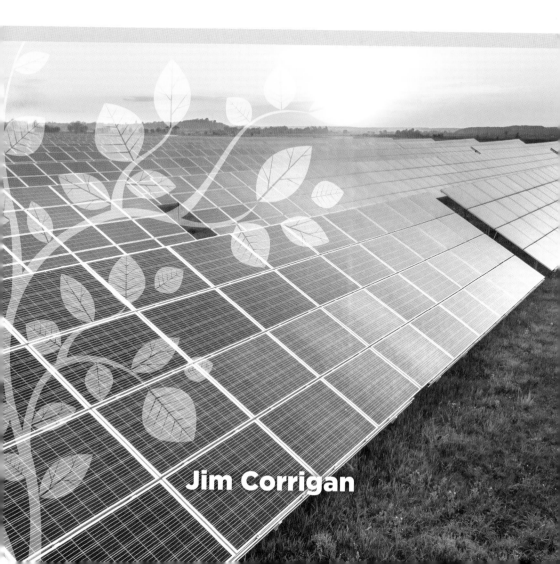

Jim Corrigan

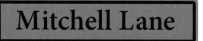

Mitchell Lane
PUBLISHERS
mitchelllane.com

2001 SW 31st Avenue
Hallandale, FL 33009

First Edition, 2021.
Author: Jim Corrigan
Designer: Ed Morgan
Editor: Sharon F. Doorasamy

Series: Biomimicry
Title: Awesome Innovations Inspired by Plants / by Jim Corrigan

Hallandale, FL : Mitchell Lane Publishers, [2021]

Library bound ISBN: 978-1-68020-607-4
eBook ISBN: 978-1-68020-608-1

Contents

Green Energy

When she was 13, Maanasa Mendu took a family trip to India. She saw that many homes often lost power. When that happened, people had no lights or air conditioning.

Mendu went home to Ohio with a plan. She was going to study the energy problem.

She knew solar panels would help, but not at night or on rainy days. After much research, Mendu invented an energy-gathering device called HARVEST. The idea came to her after watching tree leaves sway in the breeze.

HARVEST has fake leaves. When they sway in the wind or rain, HARVEST captures the energy of their motion. Mendu's invention won her the 2016 Young Scientist Challenge. She still works on HARVEST today, making it even more efficient.

Mendu is an innovator. **Innovation** means finding a better way to do something. Innovators change our world with advances in science and technology.

Farming is a good example. In 1850, two of every three Americans worked on a farm. They used their own muscles and strong animals like horses. Then innovators invented machines such as tractors to do the heavy work. By 1910, only one in three Americans were farmers. Today, it is 1 in 75.

chapter one

Looking to Nature

When innovators look to nature for ideas, it is called **biomimicry**. (*Bio* means "life" and *mimic* means "to copy.") Maanasa Mendu used biomimicry when she copied tree leaves for HARVEST.

Plants are a wonderful source of ideas. They began creeping across the land roughly 500 million years ago. Since then, they have developed many interesting survival traits.

English ivy can climb almost anywhere. You will spot it crawling up trees, boulders, and even on houses. English ivy escapes the crowded forest floor. It climbs a **vertical** surface to get all the sunlight it needs.

Recently, innovators have copied English ivy's trick. They are using vertical farming to grow food in crowded places, like cities. Often, they convert old warehouses into vertical farms, adding tall racks and special lights. In the future, they may farm on the sides of buildings.

Vertical farming saves space, water, and energy. Fresh fruits and vegetables grow near the food store. They do not need to be trucked in from far away.

Singapore has a four-story greenhouse called Sky Greens. The building collects rainwater for its plants. The water also powers a pulley system. It rotates the plant racks for even sunlight. Sky Greens produces nearly a ton of vegetables every day. Inventor Jack Ng said he hopes it inspires young innovators.

Sticky Solutions

One day in 1941, a Swiss inventor went for a hike. The mountain trail took George de Mestral and his dog past some burdock bushes. At home, de Mestral made an annoying discovery. His pants and his dog's fur were covered in burrs.

As he removed the sticky burrs, de Mestral began to wonder how they worked. He placed one under a microscope and saw thousands of tiny hooks. The hooks enabled the burr to stick to nearly anything, including pants and dog fur.

Fourteen years later, de Mestral unveiled a new fastener. It was a simple fabric tape that came in two pieces. One piece was covered in tiny hooks, the other in tiny loops. He called his invention Velcro. Since then, Velcro has become part of everyday life. Astronauts used it on the moon.

Astronaut Pamela A. Melroy is wearing pants that have Velcro patches. The tools have Velcro too. Astronauts stick their tools to the patches on their pants. This way the tools won't float away. Melroy is pictured here on the International Space Station in 2002.

World of Wisdom

When George de Mestral copied the burr, he was following ancient tradition. Humans have long known of nature's wisdom. More than 8,000 years ago, the silkworm's cocoon inspired Chinese weavers, leading to beautiful silk fabric. The Wright brothers, before inventing their airplane, spent years studying birds in flight.

Sixty or seventy years ago, the inventing process began to change. Computers came along, offering virtual space to invent. Innovators spent less time outside watching nature. Inventing happened indoors, in sterile labs and offices.

In 1997, a science writer named Janine Benyus reminded the world of nature's wisdom. She wrote a book entitled *Biomimicry: Innovation Inspired by Nature*. Benyus noted that ideas from nature have an extra benefit. They do not harm the environment.

chapter two

Human activity is hard on the environment. Forests are constantly being cleared for a variety of reasons. These include logging, farming, cattle grazing, and making room for expanding cities. As a result, we lose forests at the rate of 48 football fields per minute.

Heavy **deforestation** is fueling climate change. Forests absorb **carbon dioxide**, the main **greenhouse gas**. With fewer forests, more carbon dioxide stays in the atmosphere.

Biomimicry can help with problems like deforestation and climate change. Plants, especially, offer many intriguing ideas.

FUN FACT

Burrs are how some plants spread. When a burr catches on the fur of a passing animal, **the seeds inside get a free ride** to a new location.

Leaves of Change

In **1883,** an inventor named Charles Fritts stood on a New York City rooftop. Before him lay a row of flat panels. Fritts was trying to capture the sun's energy.

He had read the work of several European scientists. They believed sunlight could be turned into electricity. Fritts decided to test their theory. His solar panels, if they worked, would harness an endless source of power.

His panels did indeed work but just barely. They produced only a trickle of electricity. Still, it was a start. Today's solar panels work about 20 times better, yet there is still room for improvement.

Plant leaves are nature's solar panels. They use a chemical process called **photosynthesis** to turn sunlight into stored energy. During this process, plants take in carbon dioxide and give off the oxygen we breathe.

In 2011, researchers led by Massachusetts Institute of Technology (MIT) professor Daniel G. Nocera created an artificial leaf that mimics photosynthesis. The thumb-sized silicon leaf is just a baby step but an important one. Someday, artificial leaves might replace traditional solar panels. They would provide more energy and help reduce carbon dioxide.

Daniel G. Nocera, currently a professor at Harvard University, is a world leader in renewable energy.

chapter three

Spreading Seeds

Plants cannot move, so they need help spreading their seeds to new places. Oak trees rely on squirrels, which gather acorns for food. Squirrels often forget about acorns they buried for safekeeping. The abandoned nuts sprout into new oak trees.

The sycamore maple gives its seeds wings so they can fly away. Each seed pod has a papery wing, which spins like a helicopter blade. On a breezy day, these whirling seed pods can travel as far as two and a half miles (four kilometers).

An Australian company called Sycamore Technology created a ceiling fan based on the seed pod. Its single, curved blade needs less energy and makes less noise than regular ceiling fans.

The tiny splash-cup plant uses raindrops to spread its seeds. It grows a cone-shaped flower that points toward the sky. When a raindrop lands inside the cup, it makes a huge splash. Seeds fly more than 3 feet (1 meter) away.

Botanists say the splash cups are shaped to boost a raindrop's impact. Splashes travel five times faster than the drops that created them. Splash-cup plants could lead to better inkjet printers.

FUN FACT

The jack pine is ready for forest fires.
The tree's waxy cones only open in high
heat, such as from a fire. The cones spill
their seeds onto the charred ground.
Soon, new jack pines start growing.

4th CHAPTER

Leafy Logic

The city of Tokyo had a problem. Summer heat was keeping tourists away. Something had to be done by 2020, when the city would host the Summer Olympics.

Trees became an important part of the solution. In 2017, workers began trimming Tokyo's trees. The pruning spurred new leaf growth above the streets and sidewalks. Shady pavements stay much cooler.

In places without trees, the workers put up leaf-like awnings. Japan's Lofsee Company makes an awning that mimics a forest canopy. It mixes shade with dappled sunlight, just like in a real forest. And unlike a solid awning, it permits hot air to escape.

Tree shade, both natural and artificial, made Tokyo more pleasant. A Kyoto University study found that artificial shade cools an area by as much as 27 degrees (15 degrees Celsius).

Slippery Surfaces

Pitcher plants are bad news for bugs. The plant is **carnivorous**, with cupped leaves that are super slippery. Insects that land on the leaves soon slide to the bottom of the pitcher. There they drown in fluid and become plant food.

Researchers at Arizona State University have created an ice repellent based on pitcher plant leaves. Their anti-ice coating also mimics the skin of the poison dart frog. When in danger, the poison dart frog oozes toxins through its pores. Likewise, the slippery coating oozes antifreeze. It is 10 times more effective than traditional anti-icing methods.

Another slick plant, the lotus, might make ketchup stains a thing of the past. Fabric companies try to mimic the "lotus effect" for stain-resistant clothing.

Lotus leaves are covered in **microscopic** waxy bumps. When a drop of liquid lands on a lotus leaf, it simply rolls right off. Plus, the drop will carry away any nearby dirt particles. This makes the lotus plant self-cleaning.

The Sto Corporation sells a self-cleaning outdoor paint based on the lotus effect. It keeps buildings looking fresh and new. Meanwhile, a German company makes lotus-inspired roof tiles. Dirt and grit vanish every time it rains.

A giant sequoia called General Sherman is the world's largest living thing. It is in Sequoia National Park, California. General Sherman stands 275 feet (83 meters) tall and 36 feet (11 meters) across. Scientists say it is at least 2,300 years old.

5th CHAPTER

Plant Pals

We see plants grow toward sunlight, but to us they seem unaware of the animal world. In fact, plants stay closely tuned to insects and animals, and to us as well.

Many plants make colorful, fragrant flowers to attract birds and insects. Each flower is like a restaurant billboard. It invites bees and other **pollinators** to come in for food. The visitors track pollen from plant to plant, enabling the plants to reproduce.

Ants guarding acacias will sting or bite humans who get too close or nosey.

The acacia plant uses sweet nectar to bribe ants for protection. If grasshoppers show up to dine on acacia leaves, the ants fight them off. If a vine starts climbing up branches, the ants will cut it down. Ants and acacias have a win-win relationship. Scientists call it **mutualism**.

In Morocco, the argan tree makes a fruit that goats cannot resist. Goats will climb more than 30 feet (9 meters) up the tree for its pulpy fruit. Afterward, the goats spit argan seeds all over the ground, helping the tree to spread.

Plants like wheat, rice, and potatoes have formed mutualistic relationships with humans. Once, wheat was just a wild grass growing in a corner of the Middle East. Today, sprawling wheat fields can be found across the globe. Humans plant wheat because it provides nutritious food.

chapter five

Cyborg Botany

Humans and plants might be on the verge of a brand-new relationship. Researchers have begun placing electronics inside plants. They call it cyborg botany.

Imagine a rose bush by your front door with a built-in motion sensor. It could notify you of visitors. Perhaps it could even send you an alert if your cat ran out. Unlike cameras and computers, plants are natural. Their presence soothes us. Cyborg botanists believe plants also can perform work for us.

Their vision is becoming reality. Researchers at MIT have created some basic examples. In 2019, they presented their work at a computer conference in Glasgow, Scotland.

Their first plant was a Venus flytrap that could be controlled by computer. Simply pressing a key caused one of its traps to snap shut. The second plant had a tiny wire inside its stem to detect motion.

The Venus flytrap only grows in North and South Carolina.

The MIT team also made a robotic, wheeled planter. The device showed that plants can be mobile. When the researchers turned on a lamp, the plant rolled toward the light.

Cyborg botanists do more than mimic nature. They blend it into their designs. This new technology offers limitless potential.

Biomimicry is the act of copying nature to solve human problems. Natural solutions do not harm the environment. With biomimicry, people in science and business are finding tomorrow's ideas today.

27

What You Should Know

Plants spread their seeds **using wind, rain, living creatures, and even fire**.

Scientists are working to mimic photosynthesis. **It would provide energy and help reduce carbon dioxide.**

Lotus leaves are self-cleaning. **Some companies mimic the lotus plant to make stain-resistant fabrics and building materials.**

Many plant species **have formed win-win relationships with insects, animals, and humans**.

The smart ideas **that come from biomimicry have an extra benefit. They are safe for the environment.**

Want to be an engineer?
Architect? Inventor?

1. Take math and science classes

2. Enroll in art and design classes

3. Attend STEM camps and programs

4. Visit nature preserves and parks to observe nature at work

5. Keep a journal or a blog of your observations

6. Enter science fairs and competitions

7. Check out books on biomimicry from your school and public library

8. Visit natural history museums and science centers

9. Check your community's calendar for talks by science and technology experts

10. Volunteer for citizen science events like bird counts, water sample collection, and weather reporting

Glossary

biomimicry
Borrowing ideas from nature

carbon dioxide
A gas that is produced when people and animals breathe out, or when carbon is burned

carnivorous
Flesh-eating

deforestation
Clearing forests or trees

greenhouse gas
A gas in the atmosphere which can trap the heat escaping from Earth

innovation
To create or improve an object or method

microscopic
Tiny; too small to see without a microscope

mutualism
A relationship between two species that benefits both

photosynthesis
The complex process plants use to make their own food from sunlight, carbon dioxide, and water

pollinator
An animal that causes plants to make fruit or seeds by moving pollen

vertical
Upright; perpendicular to the horizon

Online Resources

Visit the Conservationist for Kids webpage
www.dec.ny.gov/education/40248.html for more information about:
Biomimicry, Green Chemistry, Green Schools, and Sustainability

Check out the Ask Nature website
www.asknature.org

Listen to Janine Benyus talk about biomimicry
www.ted.com/speakers/janine_benyus

Build your own terrarium mini-garden with these instructions from NASA
climatekids.nasa.gov/mini-garden/

Further Reading

Hawkes, Chris, ed. *Eyewitness: The Amazon*. DK Children, 2015.

Khurana, Ashwin, ed. *Trees, Leaves, Flowers and Seeds: A Visual Encyclopedia of the Plant Kingdom*. DK Children, 2019.

Koontz, Robin. *Nature-Inspired Contraptions*. Rourke Educational Media, 2018.

Index

About the Author

Jim Corrigan has been writing nonfiction for more than 20 years. He holds degrees from Penn State and Johns Hopkins. Jim became a fan of biomimicry while working on a book about airplanes. He currently lives near Philadelphia.